D1615946

Visit to an Extinct City

Book I in *The Argument of Time*

ALSO BY TERESA CARSON

Elegy for the Floater (2008)

The Congress of Human Oddities (chapbook, 2012)

My Crooked House (2014)

The Congress of Human Oddities: A Narrative of 19th Century America (2015)

Visit to an Extinct City

Book I in *The Argument of Time*

Teresa Carson

Italian translation by Steven Baker

DEERBROOK EDITIONS

PUBLISHED BY

Deerbrook Editions
P.O. Box 542
Cumberland, ME 04021
www.deerbrookeditions.com
www.issuu.com/deerbrookeditions

FIRST EDITION

ISBN: 978-1-7343884-6-6

Book design by Jeffrey Haste

For John

Author's Note

Visit to an Extinct City, the first of five book-length poems in *The Argument of Time* series, was triggered by my first visit to Ostia Antica in 2014. My reason for going there was simple: I was determined not to leave Italy without visiting an extinct city, and I did not have enough time to go to Pompeii or Herculaneum. Yet from the moment I stepped through the *Porta Romana*, the place had an inexplicable hold on me. My daylong exploration of the ruins turned into a profound experience: everything in the landscape spoke to me. By the end of that visit, Ostia was pulsing through my veins. Back in New Jersey, I wrote down the title of all five books in *The Argument of Time* without any idea what the actual content of each book would be, except that it would be connected to Ostia in some way and that the poems would have to exist in English and Italian. Good fortune brought Steve Baker into my life; he approached the translation of *Visit to an Extinct City* with the same care and attention with which I approached the original.

While there are many excellent sources for detailed information about the history of Ostia, here is a brief introduction. Unlike the resort towns of Pompeii and Herculaneum, Ostia was a commercial center that served as the main port for goods coming into Rome from everywhere in the Roman Empire. By the second century A.D. its landscape was a densely packed mix of warehouses, apartment houses, temples (for various religions), baths, toilets, bakeries, and take-out food shops. Its decline from prosperous to extinct happened over a few hundred years; by the eleventh century its marble was being scavenged to build cathedrals throughout Italy. For centuries after Ostia's abandonment, treasure hunters scoured its ruins for desirable artifacts that ended up in private collections, museums, and even the Vatican. Fortunately for us there is still much to find in Ostia. Today, systematic excavations undertaken by scientists continue to reveal its complexities and marvels.

Visit to an Extinct City

Visita a una città estinta

ominia mutantur, nihil interit

tutto si trasforma, nulla ha mai fine

everything transforms itself, nothing perishes

Ovid, *Metamorphoses*

Preambolo

Perché: sottovalutato
(anche se sulla carta funzionava).

Perché: quasi alla fine
(su "la prossima volta" non ci si può contare).

Perché: quando dopo a domanda *ovviamente hai* ...
mi dispiacerebbe rispondere *no* ...
(peccato perdere qualsiasi "da non perdere")

Perché: Pompeii (anche se senza dubbio
la prima scelta) sembra lontano quanto la luna.

Perché: un giro veloce ci basta
(2,048 recensioni menzionano poche attrazioni da "cinque stelle").

Perciò (anche se non è altro
che un mero premio di consolazione),
ci siamo avviati verso Ostia Antica.

Preamble

Because: underestimated
(although on paper it had worked).

Because: nearly the end
("next time" can't be counted on).

Because: when later asked *of course you* …
would hate to have to answer *no* …
(shame to miss a single "must").

Because: Pompeii (although without a doubt
first choice) seems as far away as the moon.

Because: quick tour will be enough
(2,048 reviews note few "five-star" sights).

Therefore (although it's nothing but
a so-so consolation prize),
we're on the way to Ostia Antica.

I

Fuori del treno: scorre paesaggio sbiadito dal sole meridiano.

    Ci sarà dell'ombra?

Una città sepolta viva, da *flusso piroclastico*—
la sua morte improvvisa, svelta;
quello che succedeva al momento di spegnere, spento;
nessun mutamento da quel momento in poi.
Quando scavato fuori, tutto al suo posto, dove doveva essere—
non un pasticcio di rimosso e riusato.
Un posto così perfettamente preservato che i turisti giurano
di aver viaggiato nel tempo al 79 d.C..

    Cosa facciamo se non ce n'è?

L'altra cancellata da *abbandono graduale*,
sgretolarsi a strattoni mentre nascosta in piena vista.
Certamente nessuna certezza sopravvive al declino sporadico.
Non importa quanto in fondo gli scavatori scavano,
poco rimane di *allora* da trovare.
Dobbiamo impegnarci, colmare le lacune,
tradurre quello che rimane da incoerente a
affidabile specchio di Roma antica.

    Sono all'altezza?

I

Outside the train: midday-bleached landscape rushing by.

      Will there be any shade?

One city buried alive, by *pyroclastic surge*—
its death sudden, swift;
whatever was going on at the moment of ending, ending;
no changes from that moment on.
When dug up, everything where it was, where it should be—
not a mess of removed and reused.
A place so well preserved that tourists swear
they've traveled back to A.D. 79.

      What will we do if there's none?

The second erased through *gradual abandonment,*
crumbling in fits and starts while hidden in plain sight.
Certainly no certainty survives haphazard decline.
No matter how deep excavators dig,
there's little left of *then* to find.
We'll have to work hard, fill the gaps,
to translate what remains from incoherent to
reliable mirror of ancient Rome.

      Am I up to that?

II

Pagato il biglietto, sfioriamo appena la necropoli—
dando retta al consiglio in una guida popolare:
non perdere tempo sulle tombe
se vuoi fare tutto nel tempo che hai.

All'inizio seguiamo i numeri sulla cartina—
sequenza di grande importanza a questo punto.
All'inizio sillabiamo le iscrizioni
e facciamo battute sulla nostra ancestrale lingua morta.
All'inizio giochiamo a Shangai con la storia—
togliendo, senza capo né coda:
la prima della *Medea* di Ovidio nel teatro
(Sì, sì, la chiassosa folla fischiando al suo atto malvagio!);
la visione di Sant'Agostino nella casa della mamma morente
(Sì, sì, si sporgevano da una finestra.
Potrebbe essere stata quella casa?
O quella? O una di quelle?);
le sei visite di Pio IX quando Ostia apparteneva al Vaticano
(Chissà quanti oggetti sono andati a finire direttamente nei loro musei?);
E guarda: una latrina pubblica da ventiquattro posti! Che ridere!
(Ti immaginavi che cagavano fianco a fianco?)

Ogni [nome] ci ricorda di un [nome] visto altrove in un altro momento.

Sì, sì, stiamo cercando di capire questo posto,
inserendoci nelle storie man mano che procediamo—
storie da raccontare più e più volte a casa.

La gita non sarà un fiasco totale, dopotutto.

II

After paying our fees, we hurry past the necropolis—
heeding advice in a popular guide:
don't waste time looking at graves
if you want to fit it all in in the time allotted.

At first we follow numbers on the map—
sequence of great importance at this point.
At first sound out inscriptions
and joke about our dead ancestral tongue.
At first play pick-up sticks with history—
removing, without rhyme or reason:
the premiere of Ovid's *Medea* in the theatre
(Yes, yes, the boisterous crowd hissing her evil deed!);
Saint Augustine's vision in the house of his dying mother
(Yes, yes, they were standing at a window.
Could it have been in that house?
Or there? Or one of those?);
Pius IX's six visits when Ostia belonged to the Vatican
(Wonder how many objects went straight into its museums.);
Oh, look: the twenty-four-seat public latrine! What a laugh!
(Can you believe they shat side by side?)

Each [noun] reminds us of a [noun] seen at another time somewhere else.

Yes, yes, we're figuring out this place,
adding ourselves to stories as we go along—
stories to tell time and again at home.

The day won't be a complete flop, after all.

[6] Terme di Nettuno ✓
    All'inizio, ingorghi di turisti come noi
[10] Piazzale delle Corporazioni ✓
    nella stessa zona,
[11] Teatro ✓
    facendo più o meno la stessa cosa,
[17-21] Foro ✓
    fammi sentire al sicuro.
[Senza numero] Caffetteria degli Scavi ✓
    non so perché.

Comincio a non sentirmi al sicuro?
Esponendomi a dei rischi?

[6] Terme di Nettuno ✔
      At first, knots of fellow tourists
[10] Piazzale delle Cirporazioini ✔
      in the same general area,
[11] Teatro ✔
      doing the same general thing,
[17-21] Foro ✔
      make me feel safe.
[No number] Caffetteria degli Scavi ✔
      I don't know why.

Am I beginning to feel unsafe?
Putting myself at risk?

IV

Enea sbarca alla foce del Tevere.

Accampamento diventa colonia.

Giove. Giunone. Minerva.

Il fiume cambia corso.

Sfami le bocche di Roma: tutto il grano passa per te.

Invasori prendono il comando, partono; pirati saccheggiano, partono;

Saraceni. Imperatori. Papi.

Carrozze scolpiscono solchi in blocchi di basalto.

Sali salgono dalla terra, sciolgono il cemento.

Fortune fatte e perse; persone care trovate e perse.

Medea—l'unico dramma di Ovidio—sparisce senza lasciare traccia,

ma le sue poesie sono trasmesse in molte lingue.

Strati di terra diventano strati di tempo.

Sant'Agostino scrive che sua madre e lui "erano protesi con la bocca del cuore".

Palazzi cadono e nessuno li tira su.

Il libro una volta amato mai più aperto.

Le strade si riempiono di macerie.

Domani non sarà come oggi.

Ordine devolve in ordine diverso.

Lapidi di marmo—iscrizioni intatte—riutilizzate come tombini.

L'assenza prende il sopravvento sulla presenza.

Ianuaria, raffigurata come una ragazza *frivola* in un graffito, appassisce in un nome
        derivato dal primo

Il fiume si prosciuga.

L'impero cade.

Il *cardo* diventa incolto.

Radici invadenti spezzano blocchi di tufo.

Crescita diventa decadenza diventa crescita—

avanti e indietro si confondono in un'unica linea

finché non vince la decadenza.

Nessuno ricorda quale sacrificio da fare agli dei per cambiare venti sfavorevoli.

Nessuno rimane a spazzare via la sabbia.

Il piano superiore dell'*insula* diventa il terreno.

Tieni alle tradizioni antiche però hai un cervello tutto tuo.

L'impronta delle strade che esistevano prima del reticolo romano

è difficile da trovare.

Animali si rintanano. Uccelli si annidano.

La connessione tra simboli scolpiti—ramo, bastone, e braccialetto—non più chiara.

Mani e menti non smettono mai di mantenere quello che sparisce.

Turisti portano via tessere sciolte da souvenir.

Vieni visto da una finestra.

Miti rimpiazzano la storia.

Aeneas lands at the mouth of the Tiber.

Settlement becomes colony.

Jupiter. Juno. Minerva.

The river changes its course.

You keep Rome fed: all grain comes through you.

Invaders take over, leave; pirates sack, leave;

Saracens. Emperors. Popes.

Cartwheels carve ruts into basalt blocks.

Salts rise from the ground, dissolve cement.

Fortunes made and lost; loved ones found and lost.

Medea—Ovid's only play—disappears without a trace,

but his poems are handed down in many tongues.

Layers of dirt turn into layers of time.

Saint Augustine writes that his mother and he "panted with the mouth of our heart."

Buildings fall and no one picks them up.

The book once loved no longer opened.

The streets fill with rubble.

Tomorrow will not be like today.

Order slips into order of a different kind.

Marble gravestones—inscriptions intact—reused as drainage lids.

Absence takes over from presence.

Ianuaria, described as a *frivolous girl* in graffiti, withers to a name derived from first

month of the Roman calendar.

The river dries up.

The empire falls.

The *cardo* becomes overgrown.

Intrusive roots crack tufa blocks.

Growth turns into decay turns into growth—

back and forth blurs into a single line

until decay wins out.

No one remembers what sacrifice to make to the gods to change unfavorable winds.

No one's left to sweep the sand.

The upper floor of the *insula* becomes the ground.

You stick to time-honored ways but have a mind of your own.

The imprint of roads that existed before the Roman grid

becomes hard to find.

Animals burrow. Birds nest.

The connection between carved symbols—branch, stick, and bracelet—no longer clear.

Hands and minds never stop trying to keep things from going away.

Tourists pick up loose tesserae as souvenirs.

You're seen from a window.

Myths replace history.

V

Sogni, rimpianti, bisogni, lotte, voglie,
sebbene una volta contenuti in quello che una volta sembrava solido, lasciano
nessuna traccia di essere mai esistiti.

Tutto finisce alla fine.
Cosa mi aspettavo?

Era un errore?
Non posso mettermi nei tuoi panni?
Non so abbastanza di te da quello che altri hanno detto?
Non posso risuscitarti?
Perché sei chiusa? Non posso immedesimarmi in te?
Non siamo simili?

Ho portato tanto da dire a questo posto
però le mie parole diventano cenere nella tua presenza,
lasciandomi senza niente dietro cui nascondermi.

I miei ricordi non sono qui.
Saremmo dovuti rimanere a casa con i nostri propri morti.

V

Dreams, regrets, needs, struggles, lusts,
though once contained within what once seemed solid, leave
no evidence of having been at all.

Everything ends in the end.
What did I expect?

Was this a mistake?
Can't I walk in your shoes?
Don't I know enough about you from what others have said?
Can't I resurrect you?
Why are you closed off? Can't I feel as you did?
Aren't we alike?

I carried so much to say into this place
but my words turn to ash in your presence,
leaving me nothing to hide behind.

My memories are not here.
We should have stayed at home with our own dead.

VI

John scatta foto dopo foto.
La sua macchina digitale gli consente la libertà di azzardare l'inquadratura perfetta.
Sebbene cerco di evitare il suo obiettivo,
ogni tanto, quando ho la testa altrove, mi prende.

Dopo, l'ora e data delle immagini divulgheranno il *quando*   però cosa ci diranno del *perché*.
Sarà facile da ricordare?

13:35:41

Nonostante i fatti a portata di mano, nonostante quanto ci impegniamo,
queste macerie non si ricostituiscono davanti a noi.
Stando in mezzo a quello che c'era, non riusciamo a dire in quale stanza ci troviamo.

Pensavo che avremmo saputo con sicurezza una volta arrivati.

Atrium? Cubiculum? Dov'è l'ingresso?
Bloccato.

Niente sembra come dovrebbe sembrare.
Ombre non cadono come dovrebbero.
Cos'è successo alla simmetria antica?
Ordine? Proporzione? Senso?

13:11:00

Cosa rimane nello stato originale?
Cos'è stata restaurata all'idea dello stato originale?
Cosa non c'era mai stata?

Possono essere, in fin dei conti, la stessa cosa?

13:27:01

Decumanus Maximus domina il nostro percorso finché non,
alla ricerca della Domus di Cupido e Psiche,
facciamo una deviazione giù per una rampa di scale alla rinfusa, atterriamo in anni di erbacce
che, a prima vista, offrono non più di un sentiero non consumato.
                                        Dove porta?
La gente del posto taglia di qua per muoversi non vista?
                Lo faresti?

Lucertola del muro scappa dietro una base di marmo.

24

VI

John shoots photo after photo.
His digital camera gives him freedom to try for that perfect composition.
Although I do my best to avoid the lens,
now and then, when my mind wanders off, he captures me.

Afterwards, timestamps will tell the *when*   but what about the *why*?
Will that be easy for us to recall?

13:35:41

Despite the facts at our fingertips, despite how hard we try,
these ruins don't rebuild in front of us.
Standing in the middle of what was, we can't tell what room we're in.

      I thought we'd know for sure once we were here.

Atrium? Cubiculum? Where's the entrance?
Blocked.

Nothing looks the way it's supposed to look.
Shadows don't fall the way they're supposed to fall.
What happened to that ancient symmetry?
Order? Proportion? Sense?

13:11:00

What's in its original state?
What's been restored to an idea of its original state?
What was never there at all?

      Might they be, in the end, one and the same?

13:27:01

Decumanus Maximus controls our route until,
searching for the House of Cupid and Psyche,
we detour down a set of jumbled stairs, land in years of weeds,
which, at first glance, offer no more than an unworn path.
                         Where does it go?
Did locals cut this way to move unseen?
          Would you?

Wall lizard escapes behind a marble base.

Non riesco a trovarci sulla piantina.
Come mai il reticolo romano non arriva fin qua?
Voglio tornare all'ultimo punto conosciuto.

Ci sono regole da tenere presente?
Solo una: la necropoli deve essere fuori le mura.
A parte quella?   Non mi ricordo.

Questo paesaggio è irregolare. Stai attento.
Gli occhi non si aggiustano a questo livello di luminosità.
Guardare giù non aiuta.
Potrebbe essere da qualsiasi/nessuna parte.

Passi rilasciano dolce degrado … cime di erbaccia punzecchiano gambe.
Muri di tufo danneggiati da radici.

Mattoni mangiati da sale.
Cemento sotto, ancora solido, mi sostiene,
ma lascia un segno ruvido sul palmo.

Fessure   spaccature   macerie inosservate   lichene   residuo bianco
brezzolina quasi impercettibile dall'ovest … o dall'est?
Aspetta, dov'è il sole nel cielo?
Che ci darebbe un punto di riferimento.
Gira e gira.

13:51:23

È pericoloso allontanarsi.

13:52:49

A John non importa.
Curioso come un micio, non andrà via senza dare un'occhiata da vicino.
Con il cuore in gola, lo seguo dentro, in mezzo, intorno, e attraverso
ruderi non identificati, trasandati.

I can't find us on the map.
How could the Roman grid not reach to here?
I want to go back to the last known point.

Aren't there rules to keep in mind?
Only one: necropolis must be outside the city walls.
Other than that?   I can't remember.

This landscape's irregular. Watch your stepstep.
My eyes can't adjust to this level of bright.
Looking down won't help.
Could be any/nowhere.

Footfalls release sweet decay … weed-tips prickle legs.
Root-damaged tufa walls.

Salt-eaten bricks.
Concrete beneath, still solid, holds me up,
but leaves rough mark on palm.

Cracks splits   unseen-rubble   lichen   white residue
barely noticed breeze from west … or east?
Wait, where's the sun in the sky?
That should give the general direction we're facing.
Round and round.

13:51:23

It's dangerous to wander off.

13:52:49

John doesn't care.
Curious as a cat, he won't leave without a closer look.
With heart in mouth, I follow him into, between, around, and through
unidentified, unkempt ruins.

VII

Non c'è nessuno.

Nessuna guardia si ferma.

Nessun cartello avvisa.

          ingresso ampio; bancone a sé stante; frammenti di vernice; detrito
Traduciamo tracce,
          taverna, panificio, abitazione
in quello che lo spazio serviva,
          mercanti? moglie? marinai? turisti? schiavi?
e da chi,
mai sicuri se le nostre teorie significhino qualcosa.

                              E se nessuno si ricorda?

Poco di quello che abbiamo letto ci aiuta molto
in quest'area di disordine.

                              Perché siamo venuti qui?

                              Non conosco nessuno qui.

Tempo passa—
come deve, no?

Non rimaniamo uniti.

                      Niente mi costringe, niente mi lascia andare.

John percorre un passaggio buio.
Io un altro.

                              Quando lo perdo di vista
                              Mi preoccupo di *non trovarlo*,
                              di *per sempre*,
                          di *essere persa senza lui*,
                          come se tenendo d'occhio
                        l'unico modo di rimanere trovato.

Le nostre parole si estinguono.

                              Perdo la traccia—
                        Dozzine di sinistra o destra,

VII

There's nobody else.

No guard stops.

No sign warns.

                    wide doorway; free-standing counter; fragments of paint; debris
We translate traces,
                    tavern, bakery, home
into what the space was used for,
                    merchants? wives? sailors? tourists? slaves?
and by whom,
never sure our versions mean a thing.

                                        What if no one remembers?

Not much of what we've read turns out to be of use
in this area of disorder.

                                        Why did we come here?

                                        I don't know anyone here.

Time passes—
it must, right?

We don't stick together.

                                  Nothing holds me, nothing lets me go.

John goes down one dark passageway.
I another.

                                        Whenever he's out of sight
                                      I worry about *not finding him,*
                                        about *forever,*
                                    about *lost without him,*
                                    as if keeping in sight
                                the only way to stay found.

Our words die out.

                                          I lose track—
                                    dozens of left or right,

                                        tutte le stanze senza tetti,
                     tanto più cielo da sognare a occhi aperti,
                                          troppo da indovinare,
                                  l'interminabile attesa di …

di?

In un batter d'occhio

                                                    non lo so.

all the roofless rooms,
so much sky to daydream,
too much guesswork,
the endless watching for ...

for?

In the blink of an eye

I don't know.

VIII

Silenzio.
No, corvi gracchiano in cima allo sgretolato
Silenzio.
No, lucertole sfrecciano nel frantumato
Silenzio.
No, papaveri cremisi sfiorano contro lo sconfitto
Silenzio.
No, un aereo scende in un turbolento
Silenzio.
E John? E io?
Silenzio.

VIII

Silence.
No, crows caw atop crumbling
Silence.
No, lizards skitter across cracked
Silence.
No, crimson poppies brush against fallen
Silence.
No, a plane descends in turbulent
Silence.
And John? And me?
Silence.

IX

Il sole pomeridiano non lascia nascondere niente.
Batte sulle cose così come sono,
come se il tempo non esistesse intorno a loro,
come se un momento fosse identico al seguente.
Il passato sta immobile oltre la sua portata.
Non può risuscitare i morti.
Non può disfare quello che è stato fatto o non fatto.

Come *vecchio* appare vecchio da vicino.
Non m'aspettavo così tanta polvere,
così tanta non-attualità degli anni passati.
Poco delle vite vissute in questa città perdura nei suoi ruderi.
Dettagli, colori e forme sono tornati
a quello che erano prima che esistessero.
Frammenti di non lascia trasparire *il significato di.*

Il conoscibile è diventato, velocemente o lentamente, inconoscibile.
La vera importanza ridotta a parole sull'importanza.
L'accaduto non può presagire l'avvenire.
Niente di inalterato in questo posto.
Ogni strato costruito sopra passato e sotto futuro.
Palette e setacci non possono scavare nel cuore.
Quello che racchiude non verrà fuori a forza.

Questo non è il mondo dove abbiamo camminato nelle nostre aspettative.
Assenza si coltiva qui.
Questo è tutto quel che c'è.
Quello che voglio vedere non c'è più.
Quello che voglio vedere si rifiuta di accettare no come risposta,
rifiuta ogni vacuità.
In ogni modo, quello che voglio non importa.

IX

Afternoon sun lets nothing hide.
It shines on things as they are,
as if time didn't exist around them,
as if one moment were as good as the next.
The past stands still beyond its reach.
It cannot bring the dead back to life.
It cannot undo what has been done or not done.

How *old* old looks up close.
I didn't expect so much dust,
so much not-there-ness of years past.
Little of the lives lived in this city lasts in its remains.
Details, colors, and forms have returned
to what they were before they were.
Fragments of do not reveal *the meaning of.*

The knowable has become, quickly or slowly, unknowable.
Real importance reduced to words about importance.
What has happened cannot predict what will.
Nothing in this place not unaltered.
Each layer built over past and under future.
Shovels and screens can't excavate the heart.
What's beneath will not be forced to show.

This is not the world we walked in our expectations.
Absence grows here.
This is all there is.
What I want to see is gone.
What I want to see refuses to take no for an answer,
refuses every emptiness.
Even so, what I want doesn't matter.

X

Oh Ostia delle superficie irregolari, dove camminarono i romani; noi camminiamo;
altri cammineranno.

Mare, sole, l'anima e desiderio indugiano nei tuoi templi.
Quali offerte votive possono portare i nuovi fantasmi a quelli vecchi?

Frammenti di affreschi, che non saranno integri mai più, si aggrappano ai tuoi muri.
La "giornata di lavoro" dell'artista deteriorata
Lui visse, il suo nome visse, la sua memoria visse per anni ma non oltre.

Ostia dell'obblio, lettere su un torso vengono assorbite dalla pietra.
Quali parole componevano? Quali frasi? Chi le doveva leggere?
Dovevano essere divertenti? Irritanti? Tristi? Profonde?

Diccelo. Capiremo.
Paesaggio dell'incompiuto, del non spazzato, della ferita aperta, dello sparito.
Oh Ostia, come puoi riportarci a prima quando c'è così tanto dopo?

X

O Ostia of uneven surfaces, where Romans walked; we walk; others will walk.
Sea, sun, the soul, and desire linger in your temples.
What votive offerings may new ghosts bring to old?

Fresco fragments, which never again will be a whole, cling to your walls.
The "day's work" of its artist decayed.
He lived, his name lived, his memory lived for years but not beyond.

Ostia of erasure, letters on a torso sink into stone.
What words did they make? What sentences? Who was meant to read them?
Were they meant to be funny? Angry? Sad? Profound?

Tell us. We'll understand.
Landscape of incomplete, of unswept, of cut open, of gone.
O Ostia, how can you bring us back to before when there's so much after?

XI

Prima, ti hanno saccheggiato la tomba:
cime dei muri, coperte da terra e detriti, colpirono l'occhio
occhi alla ricerca di reperti mobili,
(ricerca di ciò che non erano, ma di ciò che volevano essere).
Il tuo sotto è diventato oggetto di desiderio a qualsiasi
emissario papale, antiquario straniero, lacchè di dittatore, che abbia ficcato
una vanga nel tuo suolo.

Sarcofago di marmo di Claudia Arria.
Romano, circa 220 D.C., da Ostia.
The Metropolitan Museum of Art, Rogers Fund, 1947 (27.100.4a,b).

Poi, hanno sparpagliato le tue ossa—
blocchi di marmo usati per costruire basiliche in giro per l'Italia,
statue trafugate in case private,
frammenti di affreschi incorniciati e reinstallati in gallerie papali.
Quando reperti si presentavano all'asta,
nessuno ha mai indagato della provenienza.

Title (object)	*The Townley Venus*
Museum number	*1805.0703.15*
Acquisition name	*Excavated by: Gavin Hamilton*
	Purchased from: Peregrine Edward Townley
	Previous owner/ex-collection: Charles Townley
Acquisition date	*1805*

Ora, parlano per te:
esperto dopo esperto fruga tra i tuoi ruderi per una stagione o due,
poi sostiene di conoscerti meglio di tutti gli altri (compreso te).
Insistono sempre sulla tua rilevanza per le nostre vite—
come se tu ci servissi solo da specchio dentro cui ammirare noi stessi.
Passano tutta la loro vita difendendo la loro versione di te.

Colonna di Balbo: Questa colonna, di venti secoli antica, eretta sul lido di Ostia, porto di Roma imperiale, a vigilare le fortune e le vittorie delle triremi romane, l'Italia fascista suspice Benito Mussolini, dona a Chicago, esaltazione simbolo ricordo, della squadra atlantica guidata da Balbo, che con romano ardimento trasvolo l'oceano, nell'anno XI, del littorio.

Speravi che il futuro ti preservasse la memoria?
Così?

First, they robbed your grave:
wall tops, covered by earth and rubble, caught the eye
of eyes hunting for movable finds,
(hunting for what they weren't, but wanted to be).
Your underneath became an object of desire for whatever
papal emissary, foreign antiquarian, dictator's flunky, thrust
a spade into your ground.

Marble sarcophagus of Claudia Arria.
Roman, ca. A.D. 220, from Ostia.
The Metropolitan Museum of Art, Rogers Fund, 1947 (47.100.4a,b).

Then, they scattered your bones—
marble blocks used to build cathedrals throughout Italy,
statues slipped into private homes,
fragments of frescos framed and reinstalled in papal galleries.
When artifacts turned up for sale,
no one ever questioned provenance.

Title (object)	*The Townley Venus*
Museum number	*1805.0703.15*
Acquisition name	*Excavated by: Gavin Hamilton*
	Purchased from: Peregrine Edward Townley
	Previous owner/ex-collection: Charles Townley
Acquisition date	*1805*

Now, they speak for you:
expert after expert pokes around for a season or two,
then claims to know you better than anyone else (including you).
They always stress your importance to our lives—
as if you were put there to act as a mirror for us to adore ourselves in.
They spend their lives defending their versions of you.

Balbo column: This column, twenty centuries old erected on the beach of Ostia port of Imperial Rome to
safeguard the fortunes and victories of the Roman triremes. Fascist Italy, by command of Benito Mussolini,
presents to Chicago, exaltation symbol memorial of the Atlantic Squadron led by Balbo that with Roman
daring, flew over the ocean in the 11th year of the Fascist era.

Did you hope the future would keep you alive?
Like this?

XII

Ogni cosa ha la propria fase finale.
*Abbandonata Ostia in gran parte resistette * * * *.*
Il sottofondo dissotterrato;
Cos'altro abbiamo dimenticato?
*Pochi resistettero barbarismo e * * * *.*
dove il silenzio occulta le sue parole.
Chi eri diventa difficile da afferrare.
*Fango che l'ha sepolta in realtà l'ha preservata da * * * *.*
Il sottofondo dal quale sorge la vita,
Un dolore perseguita … quando era stato?
*Arte e tessuti romani sono stati persi per usura e * * * *.*
in cui seppelliamo i nostri morti,
Non pensavo di mollare.
*Le differenze non sono semplicemente risultato di * * * *.*
su cui costruiamo i nostri monumenti,
Quelle stanze non ci sono più.
*Grazie a * * * *, queste strutture antiche sono in gran parte in rovine.*
alle quali ora mi rivolgo:
Ogni fine capita nel proprio modo.
*Le case fanno testimonianze mute a * * * *.*
il libro del tempo.
Tutto quello che facciamo significa tutto/o/niente.
*Siamo nel bel mezzo del * * * *, ma non lo vediamo ancora.*

**** le devastazioni del Tempo

XII

Everything has a final phase.
> *Abandoned Ostia largely withstood * * * *.*
>> The underneath unearthed;

What else have we forgotten?
> *How few have resisted barbarism and * * * *.*
>> where silence hides its words.

Who you were becomes hard to find.
> *Mud that buried it actually preserved it from * * * *.*
>> The underneath from which life springs,

An ache haunts … when was that?
> *Roman art and textiles have been lost through wear and * * * *.*
>> in which we bury our dead,

I didn't expect to let go.
> *The differences are not simply due to * * * *.*
>> on which we build our monuments,

Those rooms are no longer there.
> *Because of * * * *, these ancient architectures are mostly in ruins.*
>> to which I now turn:

Every end happens in its own way.
> *The houses stand in mute testimony to * * * *.*
>> the book of time.

All we do means every/no/thing.
> *We are in the midst of * * * *, but don't yet see it.*

**** the ravages of Time

XIII

Quod periit,

  (Quello che è andato,

periit.

  è andato.)

XIII

Quod periit,

    (What's gone,

periit.

    is gone.)

XIV

Una buona parte del giorno è passata senza che noi ce ne accorgessimo.
Ora di andare—
non vogliamo, ma dobbiamo.

XIV

A good part of the day has passed without our noticing.
Time to leave—
don't want to, but must.

Coda

Di nuovo sul *Decumanus Maximus*,
grati per il tratto d'ombra sotto una fila di pini a ombrello,
che, ci siamo soffermati a considerare, possono trovare bis-bis-bis-bis-bis-antennati in quelli
sotto i quali Agostino camminò nel 389 d.C.

Né John né io abbiamo messo crema solare—un grosso errore.
La sua macchina fotografica è diventata pesante intorno al collo.
Nonostante le scarpe scelte con cura, le gambe sono stanche, caviglie storte, piedi dolenti
da blocchi di basalto irregolari e carreggiate solcate.
Una sottile patina di polvere riveste la nostra pelle.
Occhi non ce la fanno più.

La strada ci porta fuori la Porta Romana, accanto alla necropoli antica.
Ci soffermiamo tra le tombe che sono sopravvissute.
Tocco iscrizione dopo iscrizione, finché, prima o poi,
ci basta. Possiamo andare.

Dopo aver passato il parcheggio,
dopo esserci affrettati oltre il ponte per prendere il treno delle 18:20 per Roma,
dopo aver guardato, attraverso una finestra, il paesaggio scorrere sotto i nostri occhi,
e aver discusso dove mangiare,
la città estinta sparisce piano piano dalla nostra vista …
eppure,
eppure rimane.

Coda

Back on the *Decumanus Maximus,*
grateful for the stretch of shade under a line of umbrella pines,
which, we pause to consider, might be great-great-great-great-great descendants
of ones that Augustine walked under in A.D. 387.

Neither John nor I wore sunscreen—a big mistake.
His camera has become a heavy weight around his neck.
Despite carefully chosen shoes, our leg are tired, ankles twisted, soles sore
from rough-cut basalt blocks and rutted paths.
A thin coat of dust covers our skin.
Eyes can't take in any more.

The road brings us outside the Roman Gate, alongside the necropolis.
We linger around the cluster of tombs that have survived in place.
I touch inscription after inscription, until, at some point,
it's enough. We can go.

Once we're through the parking lot,
once hurrying over the bridge to catch the 18:20 train to Rome,
once watching, through a window, the landscape rush by,
and discussing where to eat dinner,
the extinct city drops further and further out of sight …
and yet,
and yet remains.

Notes & Acknowledgments

Notes

I

In 79 A.D. Vesuvius erupted and buried Pompeii under a pyroclastic surge, which meant instantaneous extinction for the city. Ostia, on the other hand, took centuries to go extinct.

IV

This section compresses Ostia's more than 2,000-year history, both factual and legendary, into a one-page poem.

XI

The description of the Endymion sarcophagus comes from *www.metmuseum.org*.

The description of the Townley Venus comes from *www.britishmuseum.org*.

The description of the Balbo column is the actual inscription on the column, which is currently in Chicago.

Acknowledgments

I consulted many sources but returned time and again to Roman Ostia, by Russell Meiggs, which some consider the definitive study of Ostia, and www.ostia-antica.org, which offers an extensive bibliography and links to various resources.

Some of these poems were published in the Italian Poetry Review.

John Carson took the cover photographs in Ostia Antica.

René de Nicolay did the Latin to English translation of the epigraph.

Thanks to:

Jeanne Marie Beaumont and Dawn Potter for your unflagging support, insightful comments, useful suggestions, and much-appreciated editorial eyes.

David Dear, Mary Ladany, and Angela Santillo for acting as readers and sounding boards.

Anne Fischer and Dr. Joanne Spurza, my "Ostia sisters," for staging a reading of Part IV in the Roman theatre at Ostia.

Steve Baker for bringing your perfectionism to the translation process.

Jeff Haste for your support of my work. You are generous, enthusiastic, and kind—everything a poet could ask for in a publisher and a friend.

Dr. Rivka Greenberg for your consistent belief in me.

My husband, John, for being in my life.

About the Author

Teresa Carson holds an MFA in poetry and an MFA in theatre, both from Sarah Lawrence College. She is the author of three collections of poetry: *Elegy for the Floater* (CavanKerry Press, 2008); *My Crooked House* (CavanKerry Press, 2014), which was a finalist for the Paterson Poetry Prize; and *The Congress of Human Oddities* (Deerbrook Editions, 2015). She lives in Florida, where she co-curates two programs aimed at fostering cross-disciplinary collaborations and putting art into public settings: the Unbroken Thread[s] Project and Art in Common Places.

About the Translator

Steven Baker is an adjunct professor in the Department of Italian at Columbia University and the Division of Applied Undergraduate Studies at NYU and Managing Editor of the "Italian Poetry Review" (IPR). He is also a prolific and widely published translator of texts of all sorts from Italian into English.